One Liners from GOD

Almighty Quips that Changed my Life

Patsy Moore

ISBN (Print): 978-0-9968070-0-5
ISBN (Kindle): 978-0-9968070-1-2
ISBN (eBook): 978-0-9968070-2-9
Library of Congress Control Number: 2015914793

Prepared for Publication by Palm Tree Productions
www.palmtreeproductions.com

To contact the author:

www.OneLinersFromGod.com
OneLinersFromGod@gmail.com

This book is dedicated to
my wonderful husband, Mike.
Without your generous deadline,
it would never have been
finished. I love you so ...

Praise for One Liners

This is a great book! Easy to read, very thought provoking and you can learn something at the same time. I've known Patsy Moore for many years and know she has lived this book.

Patsy is active and involved wherever she is, therefore, she has been active and involved in her relationship with God. She is a woman who didn't just want to know about God ... she wanted to KNOW HIM.

As you read this book you have opportunity to experience her journey with the Lord and get to know Him better as she did. Thank you, Patsy, for sharing your journey.

Mary Jean Pidgeon
Author of *Woman: Her Purpose, Position, and Power*
Associate Pastor West Houston Christian Center
Houston, TX

Having known Patsy for many years, I am delighted that she has felt free at long last to put her thoughts on paper, they are "nuggets of gold." This is a book you can read right through in one go, but also it is a great what I call "a dip into book," and when you do, if you listen carefully, you will hear His voice. Her "one liners" are so thought-provoking and challenging and they sound so obvious, but so many of us do not take the time to pay attention to what we hear. However, when you do listen it becomes profound. Read and be ready to be challenged I guarantee you will hear the voice of the shepherd just like Patsy.

Norman Barnes
Co-founder of Links International
Littlehampton, West Sussex, U.K.

I really enjoyed and recommend *One Liners from God*. Patsy has recorded great lessons that God has given her, complete with the one liner message and her circumstances at the time. She goes on to explain what this meant to her. Reading this book will both bless you and give you some one liners to change your life. Our heavenly Father loves us and teaches us all in many ways. I believe this book will be one of the ways.

Wes McDaniel
CEO Ideal Impact Inc.
Grapevine, Texas

I am so thankful that God still speaks, and He speaks in ways that each of us can understand. He made each person uniquely, with customized learning styles, and thus knows how to communicate with us — over and around our wounds, pains, and prejudices to get to our deepest places. Patsy writes transparently and honestly, in her own brilliantly colloquial and humorous way, to show each of us how God breaks through to get us to His purposes. There is no guarantee of an easy path here. No promises of six steps and a perfect resolution. But God's tenacious, furious and persistent love keeps pressing through to reveal Himself on each page of these gracious vignettes.

Dr. Kerry Wood
Adjunct Professor, The King's University
Pastor, Gateway Equip, Gateway Church
Southlake, Texas

Contents

Section Two

Section Three

Preface

There is a big difference between information and an epiphany. Have you ever heard or read something, and you understand all the vocabulary and the general idea, but the reality of the information just doesn't seem to penetrate your soul? That's where I found myself with God—stuck—stuck between information and epiphany.

I had Sunday school answers that were based upon truth for situations and encounters in life. However, there was no driving force within me that allowed me to own those truths. Instead of having peace and assurance, my emotions usually went to worry, anxiety, or "I've got to fix it" mode.

It was then I realized that I was bankrupt. That "love," "joy," and "peace" that God said I had was a pipe dream in my life, so I began to talk to God about my situation. This discussion began to develop into desperation as I became acutely aware that the absence of the "love," joy," and "peace" was causing me tremendous stress. At times I thought that the pressures of life and the responsibilities that I had would cause me to either implode or explode. I needed God's peace, and it was through this desperate self-intercession that God started to speak to me in a way that I could begin to "own" His truth.

I am basically a bottom-line, "just bullet the information" type of person. God knows that. After all, He made me, so consequently He began to talk to me in a way that I could "get it." I would usually be "minding my own business" or in a place of desperation when my brain would be interrupted by these life-changing one-liners from God. When I would hear them, I felt like someone was jerking me up by the collar, and then the lightbulb would turn on in my spirit, gut, or whatever you want to call it. These words became a life-changing epiphany, and God's "love," "joy," and "peace" began to flood my soul.

Often I would find myself sharing some of these one-liners in my church group or in just ordinary conversations with people. The impact that these one-liners had was amazing—not because I'm a genius, but when the Holy Spirit gives revelation to information, lives change. I could literally see the light go on in peoples' faces. God began to nudge me into writing them down, and I knew that one day I should share them with a bigger audience. I would like to say that I got busy and did it, but fear and doubt will often cause procrastination. It's been many years in the making, but God has been more than patient with me, and so now, voilà—a book!

My hope and prayer in writing this book is that you, the reader, would simply read for enjoyment. In the process of doing this, you may find some one-liners that ring "true" to you and some that might appear to be questionable. If you immediately connect with a one-liner and something clicks with you, this book will have achieved its purpose. If, however, after reading something else, you find that you're not quite sure about it, then I encourage you to ask the Holy Spirit to confirm it or not. After all, He is the best and most reliable revealer of truth. With either scenario, the purpose of this book will be realized—to reveal and encourage a real, honest, fun and loving relationship with God. If you're still hesitant about it, perhaps it would be good for you to put your questions on the back burner and continue reading. Just an FYI—some of these one-liners may seem harsh to some readers, but I know that God will reveal truth to you however you need to hear it. I usually need a 2 x 4 to hit me in the head!

The Holy Spirit is the most reliable revealer of truth.

Finally, I would like to thank my wonderful family and friends, especially those who previewed the book and helped me with the reviews and the editing. To my wonderful sister Beth, "Thank you, thank you, thank you for all your editing assistance." I am extremely appreciative for all their support and encouragement in writing this book, because without experiencing everyday life with them, this book would never have been written. I am so grateful to God for both the ups and downs of life that have caused me to both thank Him and seek Him with all my heart. My hope is that you will do the same.

Section One

"We can't help everyone, but everyone can help someone."

-Ronald Reagan

Employment with Benefits

Times were tough for our family of 5 in the 1980s. We not only didn't have an abundance of money, but we were in a cash flow crunch as well. I remember having to put two weekly paychecks together to make our house payment of approximately $425.00. The $300.00 my husband brought home every Friday was his gross salary. No income taxes and no social security were deducted. During the week (from one Friday to the next Friday) we could spend no money other than use our gas credit card if we needed to fill up the cars. Health insurance? What was health insurance? We didn't even know we needed health insurance!

It seemed that there was always something that the kids just wanted to get when we went out shopping. I remember dreading the inevitable "lane of death." That would be the section of the grocery store that surrounds you and pulls the very life out of mothers as they wait in line to check out. The zone where the imaginations of children run wild with the expected tastes of candy, the latest cheap toy that falls apart when you look at it, and the pencils and pens with Cinderella, Bugs Bunny, or The Incredible Hulk on top, all brightly colored and embellished with feathers and "gems." I would always tell them that we "couldn't afford it." To sum it up, I had a fear of lack, and I was afraid to dole out one penny that we didn't need to spend.

We were new to the Word of God, but I was devouring scripture and everyday listening to my favorite teachers on the radio. I had my four beloved instructors that I tuned into religiously. It was my lifeline, my bridge to another way of life, and an answer to our financial needs. *"But my God shall supply all your need according to his riches in glory by Christ Jesus"* (Philippians 4:18-20), and *"The young lions do lack, and suffer hunger: but they that seek the LORD shall not want any good thing"* (Psalm 34:9-11) were just two of the scriptures that I clung to and memorized so that I could begin to believe something different than what existed all around me. Somehow I expected something "magical" to happen. After all, I was told that if you kept speaking the Word and believing it, then it would happen.

Years dragged on with not a lot of change in sight. Thank God that my husband was the one who decided to faithfully tithe. We held onto the fact of *"Give, and it shall be given unto you; good measure, pressed down, and shaken together, and running over, shall men give into your bosom. For with the same measure that you mete withal it shall be measured to you again"* (Luke 6:37-39).

We may not have had carpet in our house for awhile, but all the kids in the neighborhood enjoyed skating on our cement floors, and we never missed a meal or a mortgage payment. God was faithful, but the true sense of God's richness and prosperity I had not yet experienced.

The Lord in His wisdom began to show me that my fear of lack was like a net which caught the blessings that were continually coming from heaven, causing them to be diverted from me. He also began to show me that it was the Provider, and not the provision that was important, and as the years went by, there was a change in my life from knowing "about God" to really beginning to know Him as a person and my best friend. My focus became one of connection with Him instead of the manifestation of His provision. I started to diligently seek to be one with the Lord and to live in the moment with Him.

My fear of lack was like a net that caught heaven's blessings and diverted them away from me.

Over time things began to change. Our marriage began to be enriched, our children began to get established in their lives and their own relationships with God, and the monetary provision just kind of crept in on the coattails. It was through experiencing God Himself that our lives became rich in all areas. After all, where God is, there will also be the true riches of life which are embodied in Christ (Ephesians 3:8).

And so I found myself driving back home from Houston after helping a dear friend with her daughter's wedding. I didn't just think it would be nice to help; I was compelled to make the trip to assist her. I knew that's where God was, and what He was doing. We (God and I) were one in this—a team so to speak. Noticing that I was low on gas, I pulled into the service station and prepared to fill the tank. As I swiped the credit card at the pump not thinking about the money that it took to make the purchase, I remembered the times that we could barely make ends meet monetarily. At that moment I was so overwhelmed with the goodness of God, and His faithfulness, for He had indeed blessed us beyond measure.

"Oh Lord," I said, "thank you so much for providing the money for the gas so that I could make this trip to help with the wedding!"

Immediately I heard this response,

"I always pay my employees' expenses!"

With that one-liner from God, I started to understand about His provision. It's not so much what we want, or what we think we need, but God's provision is wrapped up in Him; and where He is, there is always plenty. I learned that as I seek to be where He is and to cooperate in what He's doing, then there would be more than enough to take care of all His plans as well as meeting our needs.

Mistaken Identity

2

How does God talk to us? How do we really know if it's God, or just our own thoughts? Some of the best things that God has ever shared with me were not heard during a "quiet time," but a "kitchen sink time." There's nothing like what I call some good ole methodical "no-brainer" work like washing dishes to calm and quiet the mind. It's often during these times, when I'm "minding my own business" and thinking about nothing, that an incredible thought just shoots into my head.

As I was washing the dishes one day, I mused about the idea that many times we hear sermons on being "Christ-like" and being a "good witness." Both Christians and non-Christians will often be concerned about whether their behavior is correct in front of others. The whole idea about terms like "Christ-like" and "witness" was making me think about actors taking on or performing a role. I thought, "Is this what we're supposed to do, perform for others and simply act the way Christ would to be 'Christ-like'? Is 'Christ-like' really in the Bible?"

So, I asked God what he thought about the term "Christ-like." The answer I got just about floored me. He said,

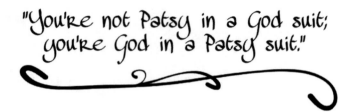

"You're not Patsy in a God suit; you're God in a Patsy suit."

I was amazed and totally taken by surprise! The thought of my person actually being one with God! The idea was radical, like nothing I had heard before—"God in a Patsy suit!"

Then I started thinking about scripture, wondering if this really was God. Does this one-liner agree with the scriptures? Then I remembered that Paul wrote, *"I am crucified with Christ: nevertheless I live; yet not I but Christ lives in me ..."* (Galatians 2:20).

Wow! I never really grasped the extent of that scripture, but then I said, "Okay, God, but what about '...*put on the Lord Jesus Christ...*' (Romans 13:14)? That sounds more like someone putting a new outfit on the same body or an actor wearing a costume to play the role of some other character."

Is there really an exchange in our lives when we accept Christ, or is it just that we have to strive to act like Him? These two scriptures seemed to contradict each other. I knew deep down inside that God's word wouldn't be contradictory, so I looked up the word "put" in the Greek. I was amazed to find out that "put" comes from two Greek words—the first meaning *a fixed position, altogether, a relation of rest, giving self wholly to*; and the second word meaning *to go down and to sink*. So, when we "put on Christ," we could say that our whole being moves into a fixed position of rest in which we totally immerse ourselves into the being of Christ

God then started showing me that I really didn't know who I was, revealing to me that wherever I went, He went. He explained that the people around me were truly fortunate, for He was in their midst because the Kingdom of God (His very being, essence, royalty and power) was literally within me (Luke 17:21).

One would think that this concept would cause a person to be proud or haughty, but it literally brought me to my knees. Truly realizing that the Creator of the Universe, God Himself, so loved me that He gave me, personally, His Son was so humbling. An exchange took place in my life when I accepted the gift of Jesus. I give Him my life, and He gives me His. As I continue to die to myself and allow His life to be more easily seen and experienced in and through me, His presence will dominate and remove the traces of my old self. There is a big difference between being "Christ-like" (with good behavior) and dying so that we can be recreated (2 Corinthians 5:17).

> *His presence will dominate and remove traces of my old self.*

What an amazing thought it was, *"Christ in me the hope of glory"* (Colossians 1:27). What an honor and deep revelation that the King of Kings and the Creator of the universe lives in me, and I have the choice each day to partner with Him. I was so overwhelmed to realize that as I "died" daily in submission to the Lord, the Kingdom of God was truly **within** me, and the fullness of God and all He is really lives inside me. What a gift I had to share! The gift was not due to the way I acted or behaved, which would be *"Patsy in a God suit,"* but it was because of who I am— *"God in a Patsy suit."*

That's the way God showed me who I was, and when God speaks truth to you and reveals His word in a powerful way, you no longer have to struggle to believe—you own it. Now when I go about everyday living, I know who I am, and as I continue to submit to God, those I come in contact with will get to meet Him.

3

Job Description Mix-Up

How did I ever get here, and what in the world was I doing? The question resounded over and over again in my head, but let me take you back in time.

I had gone to college, not really knowing what I wanted to study and ended up with an art degree. However, with three small children to educate and not enough cash to put them in private school, I ended up being a gopher/assistant/whatever-hat-they-needed-me-to-wear at our church school.

As the school continued to grow, I became more and more involved. Finally, I had a job title which allowed me to better communicate to others just what I did everyday. I was asked to be a teacher's aide for our combined 4th and 5th grade classes. After serving in this capacity for a year, I returned to working in the office with a new title—school secretary. The work was a little slow and so, with time on my hands and the memories and experience of thirteen years of private education, I began to make suggestions about the running the school to my pastor's wife who served as the school administrator.

Based on the MBTI (Myers-Briggs Type Indicator), my personality type at that time was ENTJ. To sum up that personality type, I was a "born leader." I always see challenges that need to be met, and I meet them. I am basically a "take charge" person and that "take charge" mentality was beginning to fill up my plate. I was asked to serve as principal, but opted to be called assistant administrator, which in my mind was less of a responsibility. However, the title didn't matter, the work was the same—constant, new, challenging, and often too much. The school kept on growing, and we were adding a grade each year which called for new curriculum development, updated programs, additional extracurricular activities, hiring more teachers, and dealing with the increased needs and situations of teenage students. The pool of responsibility was getting deeper, but my head was still above water.

It became evident that the school needed to be accredited to allow our secondary students to easily transfer to another high school if the need arose. The decision was made, and, you guessed it, I was in charge of this three-year project in addition to the other duties of simply running and growing the school. To be accredited, the school needed to be led by someone with at least a master's degree, so I enrolled at Oral Roberts University, doing my studies on campus in the summer and remotely during the fall and spring semesters.

So here I was, now the administrator of the school, working on my master's degree, with a husband and teenage children of my own, spearheading the arduous accreditation process, teaching three junior high English classes, serving as student council sponsor, and acting as high school counselor to prepare our juniors and seniors for college admission. Now I was drowning. If I hadn't had such an excellent principal, who started overseeing the day-to-day operation of the school, and my pastor's wife, who was such a wonderful overseer, advisor and dear friend, I would have had a melt-down earlier than I did.

The clock was ticking and the years left for our accreditation study were dwindling. If we did not get all the required paperwork and studies done in time for a site visit by a team from our accrediting agency, all our work would be for naught. So, in lieu of writing a thesis for my master's program, I opted for a project. I would spend 300 hours researching and writing our school policy manual which was a necessary component for accreditation. I would "kill two birds with one stone."

I started to eat this elephant one bite at a time. Simple—I would divide the manual into three major parts, Mission and Government, Employee Policies, and Student Policies. Having completed the Mission and Government section, I began the work on the Employee Policies. What I thought would be simple

I started to eat this elephant one bite at a time.

became insurmountable. The amount of work continued to pile up, and there seemed to be no relief. I was taking on too much responsibility, and there was a great heaviness on me. The job was too much, and to add to that I continued to cook and clean and take care of things at home. Soon I began to feel like I had the sole responsibility for the salvation, welfare, and future of 250 students. I was going to either explode or implode!

It was time to call it a day. I packed up my things and started on my twenty mile commute home. All the while, though, my mind was still busy thinking about the employee job descriptions that I was busy writing for the Policy Manual. I was just crossing the Brazos River when I heard a voice as clear as a bell,

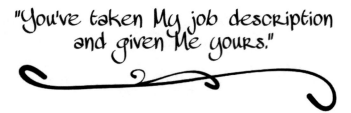

"You've taken My job description and given Me yours."

I almost ran into the side of the bridge! The truth of that statement hit me square between the eyes! God started to explain to me that yes, I needed to do the work, but I was not to take on the responsibility of the outcome in peoples' lives, and it was never up to me to bring the increase (I Corinthians 3:7) or make things happen. I was to rest in Him because His yoke is easy and His burden is light (Matthew 11:30), and really my job description was to love the Lord my God with my whole heart and soul and mind and to love my neighbor as myself (Matthew 22:37, 39). I was really confused. How do you work and rest at the same time? That's when God showed me that the litmus test for taking over His job was my peace or lack thereof. If I became stressed, agitated or worried about a situation or work that needed to be done, then I had taken on His job description and discarded mine.

The outcome: After breaking lots of old habits with the help of the Holy Spirit and a dear friend, I started to learn how to work and rest at the same time. I'm very much at peace with my life-time job description now and have no intention of taking His again!

Miscast Roles

I met the man of my dreams in college. He was two years older than I, so I took on a very heavy load of courses in order to graduate in 3 ½ years. We set the date and were married one week after I finished college. We had the perfect "Cinderella" marriage. My husband and I never argued or settled differences of opinion. Instead, we just dropped the matter. It seemed that everything was just wonderful. Our fairy tale marriage flourished until we committed our lives to Christ and started reading the Word of God.

The more I read the Bible and became familiar with God's truth, the more I knew that something wasn't right with our marriage, and the answer, I knew, was in the Word of God. Everyday I religiously listened to my favorite teachers on the radio who were preaching the truth of what blessed, complete lives we could live because Jesus died and rose from the dead. He paid the price for our sins, and therefore we were able to reconnect with God. By having a relationship with Him, we could have great peace because we know we are loved unconditionally by the Creator of the Universe.

Wow! I was terribly excited about this epiphany, knowing that I had found the answer to what had become our dire situation. I should add here that we had three children in a little over three years. Money was a rare commodity. We had to put two pay checks together just to make our $480 a month mortgage payment (taxes and insurance had gone up). On top of that, the alternator wasn't charging the battery in one of our cars, so we had to charge it every night to be able to drive it the next day. In fact, my husband had to get home before dark because the battery wouldn't have enough "juice" to both run the lights and make the drive home! We had no direction, no real purpose, and no cohesion in our marriage and family. You could say Cinderella was bankrupt. I, however, was excited. I knew God was the answer to everything—money problems, relationship issues, our children's futures, and our lives together. I couldn't wait to share this with my husband. I was sure he would be thrilled with my new information and revelation.

> *I knew God was the answer to everything— money problems, relationship issues, our children's futures and our lives together.*

Wrong. To the contrary, he was not excited about the things I was trying to tell him. He later shared with me that he was desperately looking for "salt and pepper" answers to our problems, and I was giving him "fairy dust." My husband is a responsible man who was trying very hard to provide financially for our family. He felt that devoting his time to his work was his major obligation in accomplishing this. Consequently, because there is just so much time in a day, he told God that once his career was off and running, he would have more opportunity to spend time with Him.

Due to my husband's intelligence level, it was obvious to me that surely he would get my revelation if I only communicated it more clearly and more often. I had the plan—leave books and pamphlets around the house. That would do it! Sometimes I even overtly offered them to him. *I* was getting so much out of this teaching, why wasn't he? The "teacher" in me persisted. I wasn't going to give up my crusade, but so far my plans had failed miserably, and the tension was mounting in our home.

At that time, we were in the throws of doing some remodeling in our house and had decided to paint the paneling in our living room. What an arduous undertaking! If you've done anything like this, you know that there are many steps to accomplishing this task, but this was my chance! What an opportune time to play Christian teaching tapes while we worked. My husband was cornered. I was convinced that this time he would get it! I flipped on those tapes with great anticipation, but contrary to my expectations and well-laid-out plan, he was oblivious to the background "noise." After all, he was painting, and one task at a time is enough. Somehow it had slipped my mind that most women multi-task. I couldn't share any of my excitement, and when I tried to talk about God with him, I appeared to be simplistic and out of touch with the "real world." Our communication was very difficult, and our relationship became empty.

Then we decided to tackle the kitchen, hall, and foyer floors and tile them ourselves. We had never done this before, and a friend lent us a huge tile saw and gave us a quick lesson. Needless to say, it was a difficult, dirty job with the wet saw, mortar and grout. During the remodel, the refrigerator, washer, dryer, sewing machine, and kitchen table and chairs all ended up in our living room. Our 1500 square foot house with a passel of kids, two adults and one dog was quickly becoming a zoo! I would come home from work, try to cook something for dinner, take care of the children, correct my students' homework, and work with my husband on the tiling.

One night, I was desperate to finish the floors and get the house back in order, but our church life group met that night, and my husband was dogmatic about going. He and the kids left, and I stayed to get as much done on the floor as possible. I was confused and hurt. My husband and I couldn't talk about God without getting into an argument, but yet, there he was—off to life group with me at home. I felt alone and abandoned. I started laying the tile, crying the whole time. "Why couldn't he hear me? Why couldn't he understand?" The tears rolled down my face for about two hours as I worked and poured my heart out to God. When the tears finally stopped, and I sat down on the floor in a heap, I heard as clear as day,

"When are you going to stop trying to be the Holy Spirit?"

The Right Atmosphere

5

It was December, 1984, five years after committing my life to Christ. My life was a whirlwind. I had a husband and children, and on top of those responsibilities, I had just started working at a Christian school to help put our kids in Christian education. The oil industry in Texas went belly-up about that time, and unemployment was over 9% in the Houston area. I remember always having car problems. Several times our car would stop on the way to church, and we would leave it on the side of the road and proceed to walk. It was common for people to drive by and say,

"Oh, look, there are the Moore's walking to church again."

As my husband would say, I could "squeeze a nickel until it screamed." The bills, however, continued to come in, and funds were always slim. There seemed to be no way out of our situation, and with all the responsibilities I had at home, there was nothing I could do to bring in additional money.

I would turn on my favorite Christian radio shows, and listen to them for about 2 hours each day as I did my housework and took care of the kids. It was during that era that the authority of the name of Jesus and the power of the Word of God was being proclaimed everywhere you went. I found myself consuming the Bible, knowing that the truth I was learning was the road out of our dilemma. It was our only hope! I was so excited to tell my husband of my "new revelations," knowing that he, too, would be thrilled, but he didn't share my enthusiasm. We were talking and thinking on two different wavelengths, and our conversations just got to be more and more heated.

By listening to all this teaching, I got the idea that just about anything that I prayed out of the Word of God and in the name of Jesus was going to happen. BAM! ZAP! WOW! I prayed in Jesus' name that my husband would be able to hear and understand what I was saying, that he would grab onto the truth of the scriptures, and that we could begin to get out of our dilemma. Well, no such thing happened. I didn't get my "instant miracle." I didn't get it the next day, the next week, the next month, or the next year.

I continued to pray because that's all I could do.

I continued to pray because that's all I could do. Finally, one day, in sheer desperation, I cried out to God and said,

"Do we ever have authority over a person's will by using the name of Jesus?"

In that moment of desperation, God spoke something very clearly to me. He said,

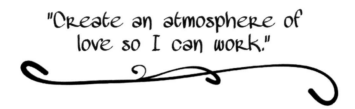

"Create an atmosphere of love so I can work."

I was floored! Was I supposed to give up being aggressive, and concentrate on allowing God to change *me* and *my* desires? Was I to give up the fight? That's when I got hold of Hebrew 4:11 that tells us that we need to strive to enter into the rest of God. God started showing me that entering into His rest and letting things go would enable me to flow and operate in His love and therefore in His power because I would be enveloped in it. He was more interested in *my* speech, *my* demeanor, *my* thinking, and *my* responding than in my husband's change. I could only make decisions for me, not him.

So it was that as I slowly learned this truth of creating an atmosphere of love, I have not only seen my husband change, but I have also seen others move into the acceptance of Jesus and the fullness of God. By bowing our knee to the Lord and allowing Him to change us, we can create that atmosphere of love, and His Word will bear much fruit and have good success.

Section Two

"The best way out is always through."
-Robert Frost

Wrong Territory

6

As I related in **Job Description Mix-Up**, when God told me, "You've taken My job description and given Me yours," I almost ran into the side of the bridge. Even though the truth of that statement hit me square between the eyes, you guessed it, I still didn't get the extensiveness of what He was saying.

I would love to think that I'm a fast learner, but sometimes I surprise myself with my ability of moving at a snail's pace with things that God shares with me. We are so programmed to think and operate in a particular way (what the Bible calls "carnal" or "earthly" and not spiritually) that we continue to do things our own way, many times unintentionally. In the process we, or should I say I, can lead a complicated, overworked, busy, unproductive and emotionally stressed life. We have nothing to give because we are so gived-out.

So, again, that's where I found myself—worn out, angry, and stressed. Where was that peace that surpasses all understanding that supposedly was mine? I didn't have it! So, I started praying. Pretty brilliant of me, really! Isn't it typical that we tend to do that last instead of first?

I knew that I wasn't supposed to take on God's job description, but again and again I seemed to do that very thing. Paul talked about this dilemma in Romans 7:15 when he wrote, *"For I do not understand my own actions. For I do not do what I want, but I do the very thing I hate" (ESV).*

It was in the fall of 1996, and I was praying desperately for God to take the "cares of the world" from me. The pressure of my job and family responsibilities were too great, and I was under the impression that I had to do "whatever," or "whatever" wouldn't get done. I mean, who else was going to do it, Santa Claus?

I'm sure that God ignored that rhetorical question, and He then started to explain how I could be free from the stress and begin to live in His peace. He showed me that yes, I needed to move my hands and feet to get the job done. However, I was not to take on the responsibility of the outcome in peoples' lives, and it was never up to me to bring the increase (1 Corinthians 3:7) or make things happen. I was to rest in Him because His yoke is easy and His burden is light

I was to rest in Him because His yoke is easy and His burden is light.

(Matthew 11:30). My job description was simply to love the Lord my God with my whole heart and soul and mind and to love my neighbor as myself (Matthew 22:37, 39).

Great! Now I was really confused. "Just how do you work and rest at the same time?"

Try as I might, I couldn't reach a break-through to that point of peace and rest. It seemed that the more I tried, the more I experienced being in the same predicament. Before you knew it, I was already down the road of stress and anxiety. There seemed to be no spiritual or emotional stop sign to assist me.

Finally, one day, when I got quiet enough to hear, God told me,

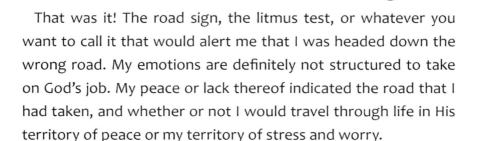

"When your emotions are out of whack, you've crossed into my territory."

That was it! The road sign, the litmus test, or whatever you want to call it that would alert me that I was headed down the wrong road. My emotions are definitely not structured to take on God's job. My peace or lack thereof indicated the road that I had taken, and whether or not I would travel through life in His territory of peace or my territory of stress and worry.

I highly recommend using the right map!

Job Title Mix-Up

I guess you'll have to bear with me through another job-related tale of woe. Once again, it was the same scenario. I was maxed out with work. School accreditation, senior year activities and the additional senior class responsibilities of college recommendations and scholarship searches caused my brain to be in a constant stew pot.

There were piles of work on my desk. Students needed attention, parents needed attention, and teachers needed attention. Everywhere you looked, there were deadlines and demands, but I would be undaunted in the tasks that lay before me. After all, hadn't I gotten the job descriptions with the right person? I knew God's and I knew mine. I was definitely "in the know." I knew there was a fork in the road, and I had the map!

It would be God's peace for me now. No more stressing out over what I thought I should know or what I thought I should be able to accomplish in a day.

That's when I walked into my office one morning and saw the mounds of work on the desk. For a moment, my head was flooded with questions. Where should I start? How should I get the information that I needed? How would I organize my day?

But, wait, why should I be concerned? I had my daily planner filled out, and I knew *I* had *my* eyes on those hills from whence cometh *my* help (Psalm 121:1)! After all, *I* was "in the know." So, I shot a quick one up to God and asked Him to help me get the work done. As I started to sit down, my movement was literally arrested by what I heard, "That's the stupidest prayer I ever heard!" When I finally made contact with my chair, He hit me with one of the best one-liners I've ever gotten.

"Who do you think I am the teacher's aide?"

As I recovered from that He added. "Rather you should ask Me to just do what needs to be done, and you would be in the right location doing those things in and through Me."

As I strove to gather my thoughts I realized, "Do we do the work, or are we channels of God's life? After all, He saves, He heals, He delivers, He reveals truth, He brings the increase and He causes things to happen. He is the great author and finisher.

All is well and good when God tells you something and even better when He knocks your socks off with real revelation. However, the revelation really has no impact until you learn how to break away from old habits, like making lists. For three months, my daily planner was out of the question. I was like a recovering alcoholic, except you might have called me a listaholic. My planner was my bar, or you might say may favorite pub, and just like an alcoholic, I couldn't belly up

Revelation really has no impact until you learn how to break away from old habits.

to it anymore. I literally went to work, still having all the things that needed to be accomplished, but I had to learn how to ask the Holy Spirit what He wanted to do. It was one of the biggest paradigm shifts in my life, and it was brought on by a necessity to get things done. It was truly a real metamorphosis.

It's been years since God shared this with me, and you might call me a recovered listaholic. I still have my planner, but now I'm free to use it all the time. The difference is that everyday I tell God that I want to hook up with Him and what He's doing, and I add what He prompts me to do to my list. By letting God be the "teacher" and not the "teacher's aide," my life has become so much easier, peaceful, and filled with fun.

Becoming Somebody

Anyone who reads the Bible somewhat regularly will begin to have favorite chapters or verses of scripture that seem to be very apropos to his or her life. So it was with me. I found that more often than not I would end up reading the book of Ephesians, and in particular chapter four. The verses began to be very familiar to me, and I found that the words just seemed to tumble out of my mouth as I read them.

One day, I was just rocking along reading this chapter, agreeing with the truth of every verse. I had no problem with the information. Who wouldn't agree with this?

1. **Unity** (v. 3) – no brainer, united we stand.

2. **God gives us gifts and talents**. (v. 11-12) – easy enough to observe.

3. **Don't walk like the Gentiles with your understanding darkened.** (v.17-18) – I wasn't going to walk in the dark. I was seeking the light!

4. **Put off the old man and put on the new.** (v.22-24) – Got it. I am a new creation; I exchanged my life for the life of God.

5. **No lying, no stealing** (v. 25 & 28) – Not a problem. My Father, God, owns the cattle on a thousand hills.

6. **Don't give the devil room in your life.** (v. 27) – Are you kidding?

7. **Work for what you get.** (v. 28) – I could tend to be a workaholic.

8. **Drop the bitterness, wrath, and evil speaking.** (v. 31) – I really wasn't an aggressively vindictive type of person.

Finally, I came to verse 32, the last verse in the chapter,

"And become useful and helpful and kind to one another, tenderhearted (compassionate, understanding, loving-hearted), forgiving one another (readily and freely), as God in Christ forgave you" (AMP). That's when I heard it:

"If you could do this, you'd be somebody."

Need I explain any further? God can be very direct with me, and that one-liner may sound derogatory to some, but to me, it was a show-stopper. I realized that really taking on the nature of God in loving others as He does makes us someone special. After all, it makes us like Him.

Taking on the nature of God in loving others as He does makes us someone special.

My Golden Calf

9

Do you ever feel like you just had to have been born messing up? You try to do things right, you try to be unoffensive, or you try not to mess up your kids' lives by the things that you do or say to them. No matter how hard you try, it's often difficult to get your decisions and actions to hit the target. The love of family and friends often compels us to strive to do and say things correctly, and yet, numerous times our frustrations and our hurt cause us to lash out and say or do something that we later regret.

Paul says in Romans 7:15 (NLT), "*I don't really understand myself, for I want to do what is right, but I don't do it. Instead, I do what I hate.*"

Sometimes the motivation to do things right is a need to be perfect, either for the approval of others or for a feeling of self-worth. The former can be motivated by pride and the latter by inadequacy or shame. When we feel inadequate or have a sense of poor self-worth, we just don't want to "mess up," and we need to get things right. Sometimes that need is so prevalent and strong that it can cause further damage to oneself.

That's where I was. It was once again a difficult time, and I felt that if I could just get things right, I could "stay out of trouble." My life would be easier, I wouldn't make waves, and things would be peaceful at home. If I could just follow all the relational "rules" and "be good"…

However, that's really not the way it works. There are scriptural guidelines, but a relationship is living and growing, so hard-and-fast rules don't usually exist. Consequently, I would get so angry at myself when I messed up. I eventually developed a feeling of self-hatred. That statement may seem extreme, but it's a subtle thing that can creep up on you. Self-hatred can start out as simply a wish to be different. From there it can develop into deep anger towards oneself, and finally into full blown self-loathing.

Self-hatred can start out as simply a wish to be different.

Sometimes the anger I projected towards myself would be so strong that I would even hit my head up against a wall. That's right, a grown woman hitting her head up against a wall. It was a form of self-punishment. You might not bang your head against the wall, but there are lots of methods of self-punishment. Perhaps you wish God had made you like someone else, or maybe you think everyone would be better off if you just weren't around? I know it sounds crazy, but that feeling of not being "enough" can *make* you crazy. It was in the midst of all of this that I heard God say,

"If you cannot accept that the cross is enough, you're in idolatry."

Needless to say, God got my attention. I realized that being angry with myself and the self-punishment that followed was my golden calf—my idol—because I was looking to myself to be righteous and perfect. I had put up an idol of self-sufficiency and self-reliance instead of simply accepting Jesus' death on the cross as sufficient for forgiveness, righteousness, and restoration. It was a misconception to think that I could ever make myself accepted by others or do everything correctly to keep everyone happy. The cross makes me acceptable and welcomed by God, and that's the beginning of everything good—a totally new way of life!

Psalm 139:14 says, "*I will give thanks to You, for I am **fearfully and wonderfully made**; Wonderful are Your works, and my soul knows it very well*" (NASB). The word "fearfully" can be translated "reverentially," which is an amazing adverb to use about how God created each and every one of us. I not only had to learn how to accept that truth as stated in the Old Testament, but moreover, I needed to realize that nothing and no one could every pay the price for what Jesus did, not only for me but for each and every one of us through the cross and resurrection.

There was no need for every action of mine to be perfect. I had been made complete through my acceptance of the cross and resurrection. Jesus had paid the price for my old life and given me a new one.

"But He was wounded for our transgressions, He was bruised for our guilt and iniquities, the chastisement needful to obtain peace and well-being for us was upon Him, and with the stripes that wounded Him we are healed and made whole."
Isaiah 53:5 (AMP)

Jesus's sacrifice on the cross has made me new, complete, and accepted by God. The good news? That idol is now off the altar!

A Grammar Lesson

10

S o, just what is a preposition? To put it simply, a preposition is a word placed before a noun or pronoun to show its relation to some other word. Still sounds complicated to a non-grammarian? How about some examples?

Let's say you make a statement like, "The ball is in the box." The preposition is the word "in." It shows the relationship between the "ball" and the "box." The relationship between the ball and the box is not "on," but "in." Even though the word "in" is small and seemingly insignificant, it makes a lot of difference when you're trying to give someone directions, location, or information. Think about it. There's a big difference if a recipe tells you to put an egg "in" the cake, and you put it "on" the cake.

Now that we've gotten that settled, here's the story. I was sitting at my kitchen counter one morning reading my Bible, when out of the blue I hear,

"Pay attention to your prepositions."

"What in the world?" I thought, "What could that mean?" As I thought about it, the prayer "God, go with us" popped into my head, and I thought, "What a stupid prayer!" I mean, if I've accepted Christ, then He's already in me. Where did He go? Did I leave Him at home? Am I not really aware of His presence IN me?

Then this thought hit me—the sermons where we are admonished to do something *for* God. I mean, really, is He that incapable? Did He call me for help when He was creating the world?

God started showing me that instead of "with" and "for," I should think "in" and "through." Think about it. If I pray, "God, please be with me when I go here or there, or talk to him or her," what I'm really doing is asking God to be around when I do my agenda. On the other hand, I could surrender to God, allowing Him to be the primary party in each situation as opposed to being my side-kick.

Ephesians 4:6 tells us *"One God, and Father of all, who is above all, and through all, and in you all."* He is really "in" us because

He lives in us. He can also be "through" us as we surrender to Him and cooperate with *His* agenda. In the Greek, "through" is a preposition denoting the channel of an act, and "in" is a preposition denoting fixed position (in place, time, or state) or a relation of rest. "In" is rarely used with action verbs to indicate motion. That means "in" is used to mean where God rests, as opposed to where He's going. It's the same as the difference between "God lives in me," and "God walked in the Garden of Eden." The first is a state of "being" and the second is a movement or action. I realized I had a choice to make. I could either ask God to come along with me, or I could live in and through Him, being a channel of His truth and love to others.

> **God wants to do His work through us, not for us to work our ideas for Him to help Him out.**

I John 4:9 says, *"This is how God showed His love among us: He sent His one and only Son into the world that we might live through Him" (NIV).* Once again, we're not just to live "with" Him, but "through" Him. God wants to do His work "through" us. He doesn't need us to get an idea so we can work "for" Him and help Him out. He wants to be invited to be "in" us and then He can be a channel "through" us to first of all bring about a change in our lives so that He can work "through" us to change the world. (You might need to read that one again!)

In Colossians 2:6 Paul tells us, *"As you have therefore received Christ Jesus the Lord, so walk ye **in** him."* We do not walk "like"

Him or "with" Him. We are not encouraged to imitate Him. What Paul does share, is an awesome truth of the fact that we are the temple of the Holy Spirit. God is alive in us each day, wanting to share with us His incredibly exciting and full life. What an awesome privilege we have to be in and through Him in His work!

Section Three

"A #2 pencil and a dream can
take you anywhere."
-Joyce Meyer

11

A Change of Address

Moving to another city or locale can sometimes be a difficult task. There are so many items we need to consider. Things like good schools, safe neighborhoods, proximity to church, work, or family often play a large part in where we finally decide to settle down. Sometimes, however, we get swayed by that "great kitchen" we saw, or the "unbelievable master bath," or perhaps even the "radical workshop" or "man-cave." What we see, and the ideas that just pop into our head often will pull us from the most important decision-maker there is:

Location, location, location.

Any realtor will tell you that the most important fact to consider for the value of a home is its location. Think about it. You can buy a beautiful house in a run-down neighborhood and you might have trouble selling it. Perhaps its value won't increase at the rate it would have if it had been in a different location, or even worse yet, it may lose value, putting you in an upside down economic situation.

And so it was that I was reading my Bible one day, just minding my own business again, when out of the blue I heard,

"When will you ever get where I am?"

I was amazed and shocked when I heard it. Who, me not being where God is? How could that be? I pray, I go to church, I usually wanted good things for people, brought a meal for those in need, and worked hard. Surely God had to be where I was. That, however, was the heart of the problem. I was going about doing "good" things with the assumption that God would be there to bless them. God, on the other hand, was somewhere else doing *His* thing. I had never really thought about asking God where He was each day, what He wanted to do, and saddling up with Him.

Jesus told us, "Follow Me, and I will make you fishers of men." He did not say, "Now, brethren, go ye therefore, castest thy net out into the sea of life wherever thou thinkest thou mayest get a nibble, and I will make thee fishers of men." Pretty blind-sighted, but thinkest thou how we go through life, day after day, doing the same thing? We are to follow Him, and the catch will be large.

Often it takes us some time to assimilate what God tells us, then to adopt those words, and finally to actually graft them into our lives. After I heard those words, I told God that I really wanted to be where He was each day and every minute of each day—easy to say, but sometimes not so easy to learn how to live.

Sometimes it takes us some time to assimilate what God tells us.

One day I was in my office, working diligently on all the things that needed to be done to take the school through accreditation, and three high school students came in. They sat down, and I asked them what was on their minds. As they started to talk, my attention drifted from them to the two foot high stack of papers on my desk that needed to be taken care of—information to get, things to read, data to organize, phone calls to make, etc., etc., etc.—and I found myself ruing the fact that I had to listen to these students at all. The truth of the matter is, I wasn't really listening to them, I was thinking about the "stack" and wishing they would hurry up and get out of my office so I could get some important work done.

That's when I heard the follow-up to the one-liner that God had told me about location. He said,

"Hey, I'm not in the "stack"; I'm over here."

No one had to tell me where "over here" was. This was not brain surgery or rocket science. He was with the students. Somehow in all His wisdom, He knew that what they were saying, what they needed, and the questions they had were of key importance, not the work on the desk. I almost got whiplash turning my head back towards them and giving those three students the attention they needed and deserved.

To wrap it up, after moving my attention from the busywork to God's present work, I was able to help the students work through their problem, and the "stack" got done faster and more efficiently than ever. God will take care of things when we get where He is. What I learned is that people are much more valuable to God than work. There was no problem that God couldn't and wouldn't solve with the busywork that needed to get done. The school got accredited, and those students still post things to me on Facebook—almost 20 years later. I think that's success, and I've changed my address for good!

Is God Really Green?

12

I have the cutest granddaughter (really, I have the six cutest grandchildren in the world), but this one you might say is very vocal. She can talk up a storm, and if you stay still long enough, she will probably tell you all the things you need to know as well as all the things you need to do. She is undoubtedly captivating and is usually the center of attention wherever she goes. If you have either raised children or have been a child, you know that there are various stages and phases of growth and development.

At one time my granddaughter went through an extensive period of saying, "I want." I soon learned that "I want" was more than likely followed by another "I want" and so on, and so on, and so on. Sometimes I would grant her the "I want," and at other times, I would forego her requests. I understand the necessity of doing that because I am more interested in her growth as a person than I am at changing her surroundings all the time.

You would think that I would be intelligent enough to translate that principle into my spiritual life, but my prayers were always filled with asking God to change things—change the people in my family, change my situation, change my location, change my— you fill in the blank. However, my life was soon to be interrupted one night as I got ready for bed.

It was another difficult time in my life. I had a teenager who was going through some trying times. I had been praying for years for some kind of turn-around, some change, some kind of relief, and just as I was stepping into the shower I heard God say,

"I'm not concerned about your environment; I'm concerned about you."

I was arrested between the hot and the cold water. What? God not concerned about my environment? God not concerned about my hurts, my pains? Could this be God? Almost immediately after these questions came to mind, I thought, "I give up on this; I don't have a clue," and because I was kind of peeved about the whole thing, I somewhat haughtily said, "I'll just pray for myself from now on." It was like I could hear the applause of heaven, like everyone in heaven was sitting in a grandstand, and suddenly they stood up and clapped for me with an uproar. The fifteenth chapter of Luke tells us that there is joy in heaven every time a sinner repents, and that's exactly what I had done. I had repented, that is, I had changed my way of thinking. Unintentionally, I had changed my "I wants" to lining up with what God wanted. He wanted a change in me. He wanted me to be able to live in a place of peace and rest, knowing that even though I may not know, He knows. My teenager's situation wasn't going to change until I changed. God was after *my* transformation, because I only have control over my decisions.

He wanted me to live in a place of peace and rest.

Jesus didn't die to change our environment. We are still in this world. He did, however, die to change us, to give us new life and to show us that He had overcome the world and given us His peace. I had to find that peace and rest because I didn't own it. I knew it in my head, but I didn't "wear it on my feet." Hebrews 4 tells us to *strive* to enter into the rest of God. That striving was obtained through prayer, lots and lots of prayer, not for others, but for me. I began to look for God in every circumstance, knowing that He would always take care of things, and my job was to "shadow" Him through every experience in my life.

My life has never been the same. This one-liner revealed to me that God is truly in control, that He loves me, and as I know Him more and more, I can trust Him to take me through every situation in my life, knowing that He has bigger and better plans for me. He is changing me, and He will change you if you give it up and let your environment go.

13

Adjusted Geometry Postulate

I n geometry we learn that the shortest distance between two points is a straight line. When someone tells us to connect two dots, we usually draw that straight line to get from point A to point B. It's a no-brainer. However, God's path isn't always the straight line, and oftentimes the straight line will never get us from point A to point B.

Life can be filled with twists and turns, mountains and valleys, and rivers and lakes that we must cross. When we are in the midst of these challenges it is easy to lose heart, to become worn out and angry, or to give up entirely. That's where I was—right in the middle of all these, believing the Word of God and speaking the Word of God, but wondering where God was. Nothing got better. There was little relief, and when there was, something else happened.

I had had enough. I was angry and tired and irritated with God for not coming to my rescue and putting an end to the situations. Then, one day when I was whining, crying, and complaining I heard God ask me,

"Why don't you just embrace the journey?"

What a crazy idea! Or at least *I* thought so. Why would I want to embrace pain, difficulty, and heartache? Sanity, however, must have taken hold, and I latched on to the fact that God knows more than I do. My concept of the word "embrace" was pulling something or someone toward you because you want or love them, but "embrace" can just mean "welcome." A dear Brit friend of mine, Norman Barnes, once shared something that really went along with this one-liner from God.

He said, "God has a much bigger plan than your present situation." He went on to explain that God allowed Joseph to be put in the pit. Even though Joseph had had this grandiose dream from God that his father and brothers would be bowing down before him, God let him go into the pit. However, Joseph ultimately ends up in front of Pharaoh and becomes the number 2 man in Egypt. Norman further shared that we don't always know God's opportunity when it's put before us, and that the "issue is not the issue." The issue is what God said—in this case it was Joseph's dream.

So I decided to "welcome" the situations, and began to accept the fact that God just might have a bigger purpose than I could see in them. I can't say that I "jumped for joy," but I decided that I would praise and thank God in spite of the way I felt. It wasn't long before I realized that if I would desire to be where God was in the adverse situation, He would get me to the right place. That decision alone caused a lot of the fear and whining and complaining to diminish greatly. By being where God was I could truly be in His footsteps. I could then walk from the mess (point A) knowing that God's better destination (point B) was ahead of me.

> *I began to accept the fact that God just might have a bigger purpose than I could see.*

Through this paradigm shift, I learned to trust God more deeply and to know more fully His love for me. His plans really were for good and not for evil. The straight line postulate couldn't get me from point A to point B. It had to be a path that wove in and out and up and down. It had to be God's plan and not mine. The situation really wasn't the issue; the issue was the Word of God and His promises. How glad I am that I listened to God and "embraced the journey."

14

Timing

Picture the Looney Tunes® Tasmanian devil. Some of you are old enough to have watched this character on TV. Others may have seen him on the internet, and others may need to google the Tasmanian devil right now so that you can follow my point. Whichever way, he was a bundle of insatiable energy—a whirlwind of movement. The Taz was always whirling like a tornado from one place to another. He was on a mission, and that was to get food.

I may not have been on a mission to get food, but I was definitely on a mission. Life was happening—a husband, three children, a home, church, and a job, as well as an advanced degree. It was crazy, and I was in constant motion, both physically and mentally.

Although this happened many years ago, I can still see the exact location where God stopped me in my tracks. I was the principal of a Christian school that was growing every year. We were putting on a new grade each year with our goal being 12th grade, so the organization and planning was constant. One day I was walking across the gym, my day timer in my hand and my mind whirling like the Taz—new grades, new curriculum, new teachers, new schedules, new extracurricular activities, and the list often seemed to get longer instead of shorter. I was becoming more and more anxious as the thoughts went on and on in my mind when I suddenly heard,

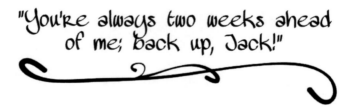

"You're always two weeks ahead of me; back up, Jack!"

Needless to say, God got my attention.

"But I'm a planner and organizer, God," I argued. "That's part of my personality profile, and it enables me to do my job. You know I can think way out there." God remained silent. There was no come-back or explanation that I heard, but I couldn't get away from the terseness of the one-liner, and so I let it roll around in my head and in my gut, wondering just what God was trying to tell me.

As the days passed, and as I prayed for understanding, the thoughts began to settle in me. God started to show me that some of the things I thought were inevitable might never happen. I was concerned and sometimes consumed by those thoughts when they might never come to fruition. I was ahead of God, and because I was in that position, I became anxious and therefore had a hard time hearing from Him. Because there was fear, anxiety, and dread, I couldn't hear God. The tension and preoccupation were drowning out any faith or trust that I had.

Matthew 6:34 (NASB) says, *"Therefore do not be anxious for tomorrow, for tomorrow will care for itself. Each day has enough trouble of its own."* That was a logical statement that Jesus made after assuring His disciples that just as God takes care of plant and animal life, so will He care for us if we first seek the Kingdom of God. That's what I hadn't been doing. I hadn't been seeking the Kingdom—the very life and breath of God and all that He is. I had gotten side-tracked. I had gotten caught up in following my own plans and projections without considering where God was and what He was doing in my life.

> **I had gotten sidetracked, following my own plans and projections ...**

I was definitely not living "in the moment." I knew that was the case, and I asked God to help me get there. I still had all the same responsibilities, and I needed to project and plan, so just how do you do this and still have peace? That's when the idea of the "next thing" prayer came to me. I just started to ask God to show me the next thing He wanted to do, and over a period of time and help from other co-workers, it became a way of life.

My eyes still had to be "out there," but as I started to live in the present, the fear and anxiety gave way to peace. I was learning to slow down. The Taz started to wane, and I began living more in step with God because I purposed to listen and "back up."

15

Quality of Life

Did you ever notice how God can randomly interrupt your life? You're just sitting somewhere minding your own business, when suddenly a divinely propelled group of words flies through your head. You can be doing the most mundane task, and suddenly there it is. That's where I was when I heard,

"Do you want to survive or thrive?"

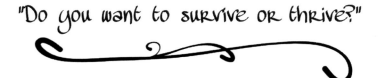

Needless to say, I was jolted to a different place. I never really thought about it. Was I surviving, or was I thriving? And what did that mean? And how on earth do I get from one existence to the other? I knew the meanings of the two words, but sometimes

I find that it's very enlightening to actually look them up in the dictionary to see what Mr. Webster has to say about them. According to him, survive means to:

1. remain alive,

2. to continue to exist, and

3. to remain alive after the death of (someone).

Thrive, on the other hand, means to:

1. grow vigorously or to flourish,

2. to gain in wealth or possessions, in other words to prosper, and

3. to progress toward or realize a goal despite or because of circumstances.

"Hmm," I thought, "both words have to do with life, living, and growth." My curiosity was definitely whetted, so I decided to look up our English word "life" in the Concordance to find out what the different Hebrew and Greek words meant. I found that there are several Greek words for our English word "life." Two of them are "psuche" and "zoe."

Psuche has to do more with our soul—what we think, what we want, and what we feel. It involves the breath of life that allows us to be a living soul, to walk, to talk, to breathe. It encompasses our personality and our human character traits. This word is used in Matthew 6:25 when Jesus says, *"Therefore*

I tell you, do not worry about your life, what you will eat or drink ..." (NIV). "Life" here means that living soul or being.

Zoe, however, has a different connotation. This life is generally considered to be eternal life or the very life of God, a life that is active, vigorous, and animate. This life has to do with our spirit. In John 10:10 Jesus said, "*... I am come that they might have life and have it more abundantly.*" This had to be something different. Jesus wasn't in a cemetery talking to a bunch of dead bodies. He was speaking to a bunch of living, breathing "psuches." He wouldn't have said such a thing unless He had another type of life for us—His life.

So I thought, "Well, that makes sense. I can sit here, surviving the everyday activities of mere existence, or I can have a life like Jesus." Think about it. His day was filled with activity (people being healed), excitement (dead bodies coming back to life) and purpose (sharing truth and life with those He met). He never went backwards, always forwards, even when He was going to the cross. There was always a goal, He knew what it was, and He pursued it with gusto. In fact, Jesus thrived so much that life literally exuded out of Him. The woman who touched the hem of His clothes was instantly healed because that life went

There was always a goal, He knew what it was, and He pursued it with gusto.

out of Him to her, energizing and making her whole! The more I thought about thriving vs. surviving, the more evident it became that I wanted to experience that "zoe" life. By just surviving, I had limited vision for my present and future, but if I chose to thrive, the possibilities were endless.

So how was I to move from just surviving to thriving? We only need food and water to survive. We can be a blob of "living mass" on the outside by simply eating and drinking, maybe going to work and doing the ordinary mundane things of life, but this will not cause us to thrive. The catalyst that causes us to get from surviving to thriving is a sold-out relationship with God through Jesus with the Holy Spirit filling our lives with God's love, wisdom and direction. Jesus is our example. He had to lay down his psuche (Matthew 2:28) so that we could have the zoe life of God (John 10:10). He had to be sold-out to the Father to live this way and to go to the cross, no matter how difficult, so that we could be heirs to a thriving life—His very life!

> **To get from surviving to thriving requires a sold-out relationship with God.**

To keep ourselves in the thriving mode, however, we must also pay strict attention to our diet. Jesus said for us to come to Him if we were thirsty (John 7:37). Hanging around with Jesus can slake that thirst that mere survival causes us to have. As for food, man cannot live by burgers alone (liberty taken here), but by the very Word of God. In scripture we find that the Word of God is equated to milk and meat (1 Corinthians 3:2)—suitable foods for the new Christian and the more mature believer, but then, these are only the staples of the God kind of life. "Where is the dessert?" you might ask. You don't need to look any further. The Word of God is described as being sweeter than honey (Psalm 119:103). Jesus Himself, the living, breathing Word of God, tops off the meal and leaves you feeling more than satisfied. That dessert is an eternal treat! Last, but not least, to thrive instead of survive, be sure that your list of dinner companions regularly includes those that know how to eat the best things that God has to offer.

Section Four

"Whatever you do in life, make
sure it is big, even if it's just
washing elephants."

-Louis J. Mathieu

Insurance Magnate & Oil Tycoon

(otherwise known as my Uncle Louie)

16

The Great Spirit

It was the fall of 1984. I was homeschooling our children, and we had been working on social studies. The weather was changing, and the oppressive heat of Houston was being driven out by the welcome cool fronts. Ideas of pumpkins, Thanksgiving, Indians and Pilgrims filled our minds as the weather continued to change. I do believe that those of us who experience oppressively hot summers focus on these things so much more.

I had decided to take a break from school and sent the children out to play and enjoy the cooler weather. They immediately bee-lined to their favorite tree and soon became engrossed in being monkeys. I was watching them go from limb to limb when I heard:

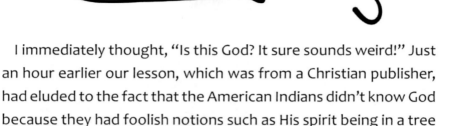

"The American Indians knew more than my Church; I am in the tree."

I immediately thought, "Is this God? It sure sounds weird!" Just an hour earlier our lesson, which was from a Christian publisher, had eluded to the fact that the American Indians didn't know God because they had foolish notions such as His spirit being in a tree or other forms of nature. Here were two opposite opinions— one that I had read in a Christian book, and one, that I felt very strongly, came from God.

So, how was I to reconcile this dilemma? On the one hand, I had the general, traditional "Christian concept." On the other hand I had something that I thought God had told me, and yet it sounded almost pantheistic. Was I going to believe that the essence of God is in all things? Trying to get around this one-liner made me think of the futility of the proverbial argument of the number of angels on the top of a pin! Where was I to start? So I asked God to show me how this worked if what I heard was really from Him.

I started to think and read about the creation account in the Bible. It is evident to most people that, according to scripture, most of creation was formed only through God's spoken words. He used "let" and "let there be" over and over, so the following scriptural deductions went through my head.

God spoke words when He created. When He spoke, His breath came forth out of Him, and creation appeared just as He said it. After God formed man out of the dust of the earth, He *"breathed into his nostrils the breath of life"* (Genesis 2:7). The breath of God brought forth life on the earth. God didn't have a tank of life with a hose attached to it to bring life into the world, but rather the life came out of Him. There was no other life at the time. He was the artist, creating His masterpiece, and just like da Vinci or Michelangelo whose art is considered to be expressions of the artists themselves, so is creation an expression of God—indeed His very being and life. In fact, in John 1, Jesus is called the "Word" which means an expression of a thought, and in this case He is the Divine expression or the embodiment of the nature of God the

> **God didn't have a tank of life with a hose attached to it to bring life into the world, but rather the life came out of Him.**

Father Himself. Paul put it this way in Romans 1:19-20, *"since what may be known about God is plain to them, because God has made it plain to them. For since the creation of the world God's invisible qualities—his eternal power and divine nature—have been clearly seen, being understood from what has been made, so that people are without excuse"* (NIV). In other words, when we look at creation, it is evident that there is a God because you can see His very being in what He has created.

"Yes," I thought, "God is in the tree!" I know that I'm not going to bow down and worship a tree, because there is a *God* who made all this beauty possible through His breath and His words.

This master Creator not only exists in the tree and the rest of creation, but He's also separate from it.

Now, my intention is not to get too weighty with this or to split hairs over this. I encourage you, if you're the curious type, to ask God for yourself about His presence in His creation. The answer that you get from Him may change your life. I know your grocery shopping and walks on a beautiful day will be different. When you do these ordinary things, you may be surprised to find yourself marveling at the expression of God that you see—the colors, shapes, smells, and tastes that He has blessed us with that we might get a better idea of His true majesty!

The Divine Developer

I t had not been a long time since I committed my life to Christ. I remember after walking forward and making that commitment, I experienced a download of understanding and revelation about God. It was like all the things that I learned about God when I was growing up got "dumped" from my head to my heart, and I began to see things differently. Shortly after this event, I realized something was wrong in our family. This had me puzzled because my husband and I never fought, and we had beautiful, healthy children. We had a comfortable home, and although we didn't have a lot of money, the bills were paid.

As the weeks went by, I realized that there was something wrong with my husband's and my relationship. I really didn't even know what it was, but when I started reading the Word of God, I just sensed in my gut that our home was out of order. How do you make any sense of this? As I started reading more and more in my Bible, I began to see what I really wanted in a husband. Trust me, he was very good-looking, but I really yearned to have that love of God in my marriage between us, and I wanted to follow someone who followed God closely and had lots of Godly wisdom.

I happened to hear Campbell McAlpine teach one time, and he opened my eyes to praying the words of God for people. I knew this was what I wanted to do for my husband. Every day I would read scriptures with his name in it instead of "the man" or "the one." Psalm 1:1-3 was a regular. I wanted a husband who was wise and whose "delight was in the law of the Lord," because "whatever he did would prosper," and of course that would be good for all of us.

I saw some changes, but I was impatient. *I* wanted more and *I* wanted it faster! One morning when I was talking to God, or should I say whining about my situation, I heard,

"Why do you keep looking to see if the bathroom is clean; why not just enjoy the clean living room?"

No one needed to interpret that for me! God was trying to get my focus off of what wasn't to what was. Immediately I thought about, *"Do not despise these small beginnings, for the Lord rejoices to see the work begin ..."* (Zechariah 4:10). Zechariah was writing about the beginning of rebuilding the temple. How apropos for God to bring this scripture to my mind! God is building a temple in all of us. As we cooperate with Him, He is constantly changing us, developing us, and making us complete. This is what He was doing in my husband and also in me.

God isn't looking at us to see our flaws and imperfections. He sees us with the eyes of a loving Father who has unconditional love. He sees our potential, because He really knows the impact of redemption. He rejoices in our small steps toward being who He has called us to be. He is the perfect Father.

> *He rejoices in our small steps toward being who He has called us to be.*

So how did this one-liner impact my life? I had to learn to have patience, love, trust in God, and joy in the midst of the situation. I had to start seeing the glass half full instead of half empty, and I had to pray that God would give me a grateful heart. I can't say that I "arrived" through this experience, but it was the beginning of God's teaching me to see things differently—maybe like He does?

To Jingle or Not to Jingle?

When I was growing up, I remember that everyone came to our house for holidays, football games, and various celebrations. Much time was spent shopping, cooking, and decorating the tables, always using the best china and silver. It was exciting! I would see my aunts and uncles, friends, and other relatives, and I would love to just hang out, eavesdrop, and watch the interaction of our family. It was a gift. We were rich in that we shared life so fully.

After committing my life to Christ as an adult, I started attending church at a different denomination than the one in which I was raised. I was green, and I do mean kelly green! My knowledge of scripture was limited, my "Christianese" (the terms that some Christians use that no one else understands) was nonexistent, and my information about the "do's" and "don'ts," when compared to that of the congregation, was bankrupt. I had no clue! However, I was impressed with the general knowledge of scripture and the faith of those around me, and questions that I had always had were being answered little by little.

Fall had arrived, and thoughts of the upcoming holiday celebrations were running through my head. We had a tradition of going to Oklahoma for Thanksgiving and New Orleans for Christmas, being with the different sides of the family for the two celebrations. It was something the children looked forward to all year. In fact, all our children and their cousins on my husband's side of the family (there were 11 altogether), began calling Thanksgiving "the love feast." That's when the bomb dropped.

I started hearing people around me in the church saying that they didn't believe it was right to have a Christmas tree, Christmas lights, or other decorations. Many didn't give gifts, and they felt that anything outside of "church" was making Christmas a commercial event. I was literally floored! Had I been doing things wrong all this time? I respected the people I had met in the church, and I held their opinions in high regard. I surely didn't want to do something wrong and offend God, but then it was so different than the way I grew up. I was in a quandary, and then I had an epiphany (better late than never)! Why not ask God what *He* thinks? That's when I heard these words.

"The Church could learn something from the world when it comes to celebrating my birth."

I thought I needed to clean out my ears! I asked God a question, and here it was again, something contrary to what I was hearing among "churched" people. However, as I started to think about it, what God told me really started to make sense. Think about all the brouhaha that is associated with commercialized Christmas. First, retailers ponder what they will stock and the sales that will run for months before December. It's part of their marketing agenda. Plans are made, additional people are hired, and advertisement is developed. Then we get the commercials for what seems like years before December 25. Christmas decorations start arriving in the stores around the end of August, and if you need a string of Christmas lights in December, you may be out of luck because they're all sold out.

The baking, the invitations, the parties, the cards, the well-wishes, the anticipation of family, friends, and food. Is this so terrible? Doesn't this sound like what should be more of a Christ-follower's way of life? Shouldn't we be thinking of others, how we can give to them, words of encouragement and well-wishes, opening our homes to others, and creating an environment where people want to come and share time together?

Even though the dollar-driven commercialism of Christmas has become common place, there is still a reason that they do it in December. It's not the January White Sale, it is the **CHRIST**mas sale. Even if the world doesn't believe in God, much less Jesus, why do they even do what they do? Whether they want to admit it or not, every sale, every advertisement, every ornament, and every mobile, talking, and flying reindeer are all attestations of the birth of Christ! They wouldn't be able to make the

Isn't God brilliant to allow all this to happen just to draw attention to His Son, Jesus?

bucks if it weren't for His birth. Even the most passionate Nativity-scene-removing activist doesn't go to work on Christmas. He or she gets to stay home and have turkey because of Jesus. Isn't God brilliant to allow all this to happen just to draw attention to His Son, Jesus?

No other holiday of the year, anywhere in the world evokes so much commotion and celebration as Christmas. Whether someone knows it or not, he or she gets to celebrate this holiday because *"God so loved the world that He gave His only begotten Son, that whosoever believes in Him should not perish but have everlasting life"* (John 3:16).

We do it up at our house at Christmas. Celebrate with good food, friends, and parties, rejoicing in the awesome truth of the season—of the incredible Gift that was given to us that we might have a full, complete life, being a friend of God. Because God gave, we can be someone new, a new creation, perfect and right-standing in His eyes. Don't you think it's worth killing the Christmas goose over that?

19

No Daddy Warbucks

When my husband and I relocated to the Dallas-Ft. Worth area, God provided an amazing house for us. We had lived in a smallish 1500 square foot house in Houston and had raised our children there. Sometimes things would get really hectic. It's quite difficult to have two teenage daughters with polarized habits and personalities sharing a small bedroom. I often pondered over how my husband and I would give them our master bedroom and we'd take theirs, or another idea was to get rid of the washer and dryer, stick a small mattress and box spring in there, and suck it up and go to the laundromat. I was tempted. The solutions sometimes seemed so much better than the existing situation.

Anyway, as one would say, "I digress." Our new house was wonderful with lots of space, multiple air conditioning units to conserve energy and money, and a great quiet location. However, the decorating and some of the layout didn't quite fit our taste and lifestyle, so we had done some remodeling over the years. I love to design and decorate. It's something that comes easy to me—guess it's just a gift that God has given me. Our family isn't afraid to tackle things, and so we raised some doorways, put up new headers, and painted. Some things, however, we did leave to the experts.

Our master bath is large. In fact, the two bedrooms that our children had in Houston could fit in it. But with a large bathroom comes more work, and it was not fun to clean. (Come to think of it though, I never really consider cleaning as being fun.) There was so much counter space that we didn't need, large mirrors on three walls, a bathtub that could hold 5 toddlers, pink tile, and roses etched on the shower glass. The first four of those had to do with cleaning, the last two are not my taste. I really wanted to do something with the bathroom.

Because my mind went to "It ain't broke, so don't fix it," I had a hard time justifying this desire. I also considered the money that it would cost. Consequently, I spent a lot of time praying about it, wondering if I should cough up the cash. I was sitting in the kitchen one morning talking to God about my dilemma (the decision on remodeling the bathroom), and I asked Him, "God, is it prudent to do that?" Almost before I finished my question, I was interrupted with,

"I'm not prudent; I'm lavish."

Stunned again! He got me. It's like I was expecting something like "No" or "It's okay" or "What do you want?" Instead God hit me with a truth about Himself that transcended the question. God is lavish. As He further explained,

"I'm not prudent. Look at creation. What do you think it would look like if I had been 'prudent'? Rather, you should ask if that's where I'm going."

The thought occurred to me that God really doesn't peel the bucks out of His extremely large wallet. He *is* the provision, and therefore, where He *is*, there will *be* the provision. It's that simple. Needless to say, this time with God and this one-liner radically changed my perspective on how I should walk forward in life, and how decisions should be made. I purposed to always ask God if He was where I thought I should go or what I thought I should do.

> *He is the provision. Where He is, there will be the provision.*

The bathroom did get remodeled, and I love it. More than just enjoying the way it looks, I always remember my conversation with God when I go into that room. God wasn't that concerned about the remodel of the bathroom. He was more interested in my remodel. He wanted me to know His nature and who He is more deeply than I had known before. I learned the real value of including God in all we do and in all we experience. The stuff isn't that important, and the remodels eventually become outdated, but my relationship with Him becomes sweeter and sweeter.

Housekeeping

In the summer of 1983, I decided to pull my two older children out of public school and home-school them. I was also going to teach my youngest, but since she had just turned five that year, she had not as of yet been in school. My college background was in art, but after all, the kids were in elementary grades and kindergarten. "It couldn't be that difficult," I mused.

How exciting this was! The kids couldn't believe that "they didn't have to go to school." I was ordering curriculum, we were buying school supplies, and all three of them thought that it would be great to learn math while in their pajamas if they wanted to. I had decided to more or less adhere to the annual calendar for the local school district so that the kids could continue to play with all their pals on the street. So, when the first day of school rolled around, and the carpool left our neighborhood, we went to our schoolhouse—the kitchen table.

All this was new to me. I had never made lesson plans or thought about teaching one child, much less three. I soon decided to put my second grade son into third grade social studies and science with his older sister just to make my life a little more doable. It wasn't so doable for him at first, but I thought it made perfect sense for *me*. I poured over the study guides and followed them like they were my Bible. I felt like I had to do all the activities that were suggested for teachers. Did *I* know the suggestions were options? Needless to say, I treated them like they were the law. I would stay up late at night making all the cut-out fish so they could "trawl" for the right vowel sounds, I made the game boards, and I even made the phonics beanbag toss. I was putting so much pressure on myself. Every moment of my day seemed to be filled to capacity, and still I was worried that I wasn't going to do a good enough job. Thoughts filled my head about their not doing well and having to repeat the grade in school the next year. The pressure was mounting.

Because I wanted my children to understand the discipline of organization, I had certain requirements. They were to have their homework in folders ready to hand in, and they were to pack their books and bring their supplies to our "school" the next morning. I felt it was necessary to do this in case I ever decided to enroll them in either a public or private school again.

One morning, shortly after 9:00 a.m. (which was when our school started), all four of us were sitting around the kitchen table. I can see it like it was yesterday. All three of my children were dressed, ready and eager to learn, and looking at me with expectant eyes. It was then, as I looked into their eyes, that I became conscious of something that would literally change my life. Out of the blue, as I looked at each one of my children, I realized even though they were only 8, 7, and 5 years old, they had all accepted Christ. The truth of the matter was that they had each exchanged his or her life for Christ's life because of the new birth. "Oh my!" I thought. "That's Jesus, and Jesus, and Jesus. What am I going to teach Jesus?"

Immediately I felt totally inadequate. I knew they needed to learn things, and I was there to teach them; but the reality of their new lives was so predominant. Because I really didn't know what to do at that moment, I "closed the school" and sent them out to play with the P.E. teacher who was our dog. The only thing I could do was pray, so I went to my room and asked God, "How do you do this? How do I teach Jesus?" Right then and there I heard,

"Dust off the light bulb."

As crazy as that sounds, I knew immediately what God meant. Teaching them wasn't what I was going to pour in their heads, but rather I was to love them and to meet their needs and to teach them to think like God does according to His word. This would clean up the dust and the cobwebs, and the light of God would shine in them, allowing them to really learn as opposed to having brains that are overloaded with information. Knowledge is really the lowest level of education. Proverbs is riddled with references to knowledge, understanding, and wisdom. Knowledge is simply the state of knowing facts; understanding, on the other hand, is discernment, comprehension, and interpretation; and finally wisdom is the capacity to make use of knowledge to the best ends and the best means. Wisdom encompasses discretion, skill, discernment, and judgment.

Now I had direction, and I had a plan—get out the dust rag. I can't say that I did everything right, but because I hooked up with God's plan, He did it right. Today, my three children are all grown with families of their own. I'm not proud because of what they have done or of what they are presently doing. I am proud because of who they are. I am, however, more than impressed with their many accomplishments. What a success they are today—in their minds, their emotions, and relationships with friends, family, and especially God! They are not perfect by any means, but they are all grounded and established because they know who they are and they continue to learn how much God loves them. They have moved from knowledge to understanding, to wisdom. I know that listening to God and "dusting off the light bulbs" had something to do with it. For this one-liner, I am most grateful.

They are not perfect, but they are all grounded and established in the knowledge of who they are.